You Are the Light of the World

A Bible Quotes Journal
to Guide and Inspire

STERLING CHILDREN'S BOOKS
New York

An Imprint of Sterling Publishing Co., Inc.
1166 Avenue of the Americas
New York, NY 10036

ISBN 978-1-4549-2838-6

Distributed in Canada by Sterling Publishing Co., Inc.
c/o Canadian Manda Group, 664 Annette Street
Toronto, Ontario, M6S 2C8, Canada
Distributed in the United Kingdom by GMC Distribution Services
Castle Place, 166 High Street, Lewes, East Sussex, BN7 1XU, England
Distributed in Australia by NewSouth Books
45 Beach Street, Coogee, NSW 2034, Australia

For information about custom editions, special sales, and premium and
corporate purchases, please contact Sterling Special Sales at 800-805-5489 or
specialsales@sterlingpublishing.com.

Manufactured in Canada

Lot #:
2 4 6 8 10 9 7 5 3 1
12/17

sterlingpublishing.com

Bible verses courtesy of the *Bible in Basic English*

Cover and interior design by Irene Vandervoort
Cover and interior illustrations by Flora Waycott

The artwork in this book was created using mixed media.

You Are the Light of the World

A Bible Quotes Journal to Guide and Inspire

ILLUSTRATED BY FLORA WAYCOTT

STERLING CHILDREN'S BOOKS
New York

Throughout life's struggles, God can bring comfort and reassurance to those who look to Him. In times of blessings, we celebrate Him with gratitude. The quotes in this journal offer a timeless reminder of God's teachings and the love He spreads with His word. Here, you can reflect, problem-solve, or write down your goals, all the while inspired by encouraging and uplifting Biblical passages. Whether you're planning your future or recording your present, this is a place for you to express yourself alongside inspiring reminders of God's teachings.

God's light shines through the quotes on these pages and will help you illuminate your own writings with kindness, justness, and clarity. Even in the darkest times, guiding your thoughts with the everlasting wisdom of the Lord can show you the way to a brighter life!

The desire
of the upright man
is only for good,
but wrath is waiting
for the evil-doer.

PROVERBS 11:23

Love is never tired of waiting;
love is kind; love has no envy; love
has no high opinion of itself,
love has no pride; Love's ways are
ever fair, it takes no thought for
itself; it is not quickly made angry,
it takes no account of evil; It takes
no pleasure in wrongdoing, but has
joy in what is true; Love has the
power of undergoing all things,
having faith in all things,
hoping all things.

1 CORINTHIANS 13:4–7

My loved ones,
let us have love for one
another: because love is
of God, and everyone
who has love is a child
of God and has
knowledge of God.

1 JOHN 4:7

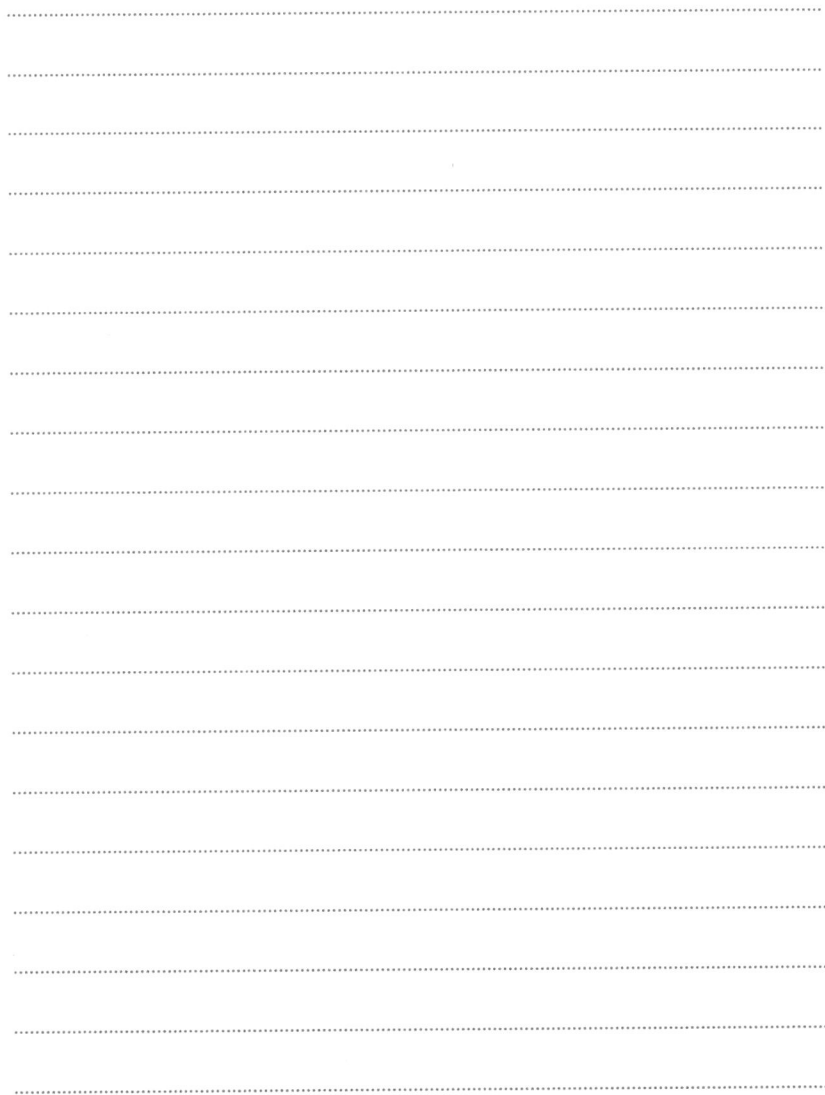

But the fruit
of the Spirit is
love, joy, peace, a
quiet mind, kind acts,
well—doing, faith,
gentle behavior,
control over desires:
against such there
is no law.

GALATIANS 5:22–23

March 14, 2021

I like this rendition of the bible verse.
It helps show the difference from "goodness
and kindness". It doesn't flow as well,
but it's more descriptive. I need peace
right now, God. I'm having trouble seeing
you and putting my faith in you. I know
I shouldn't be soley driven by emotion and
whether or not I feel your presence, but
it still feels discouraging. Is this a test?
Maybe I'm too focused on material items...
or my relationships! Do I truly believe I'll
be okay without Tristan - if that doesn't work
for us in the future? Why do I feel so
distant to you God? Maybe I have Daddy issues.
I think I'll try the 30 days w/ Jesus study
plan. I want to work harder at this. I
don't think I'm truly giving my best. Guide
me, God. I need your comfort. Am I doing well?

I have said
all these things to
you so that in me
you may have peace.
In the world you
have trouble;
but take heart!
I have overcome
the world.

JOHN 16:33

Now the Lord of peace
himself give you
peace at all times
and in every way.
May the Lord
be with you all.

2 THESSALONIANS 3:16

I am of the
opinion that there
is no comparison
between the pain
of this present time
and the glory which
we will see in
the future.

ROMANS 8:18

The end of a thing
is better than its start,
and a gentle spirit is
better than pride.

ECCLESIASTES 7:8

But in
the Writings it says,
He who puts in only
a small number of seeds,
will get in the same;
and he who puts them
in from a full hand, will
have produce in full
measure from them.

2 CORINTHIANS 9:6

For God is true and
will not put away
from him the memory
of your work and
of your love for his name,
in the help which
you gave and still give
to the saints.

HEBREWS 6:10

Yes, though I go
through the valley
of deep shade,
I will have no fear
of evil; for you are
with me, your rod
and your support
are my comfort.

PSALM 23:4

Keep yourselves
in the fear of the Lord,
all you his saints;
for those who do so
will have no need
of anything.

PSALM 34:9

So will
your delight
be in the Lord,
and he will
give you your
heart's desires.

PSALM 37:4

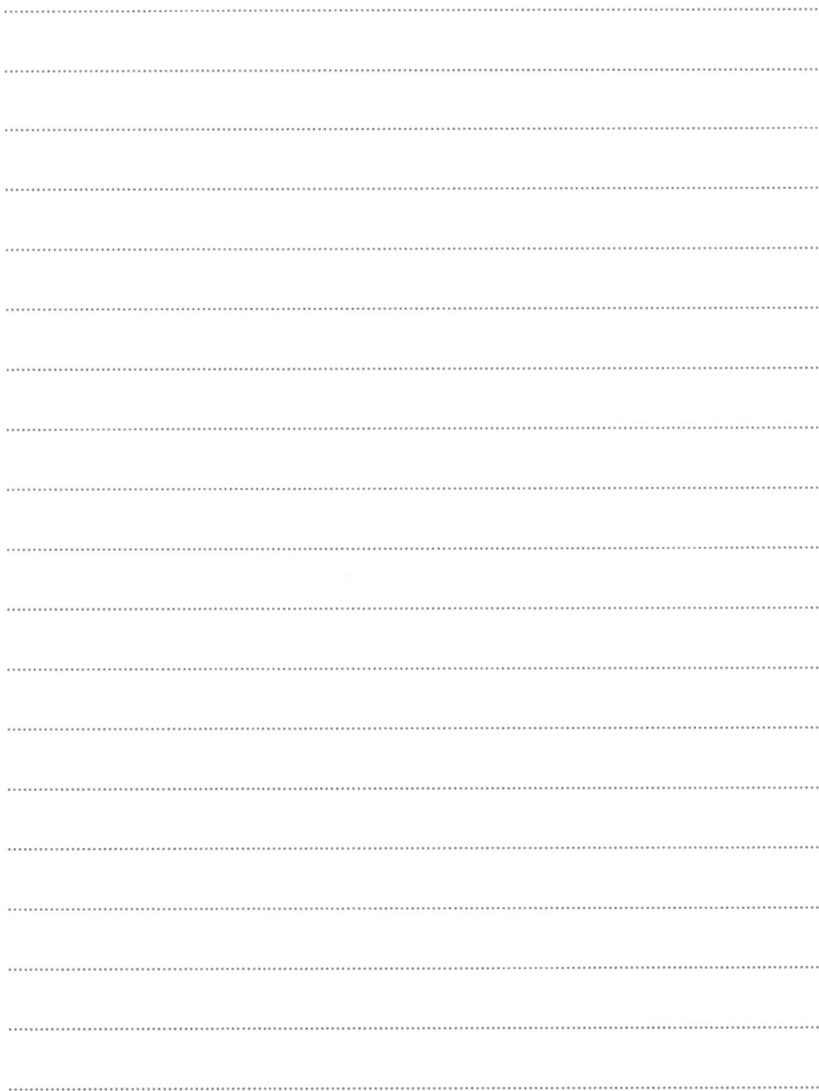

But those
who are waiting
for the Lord will
have new strength;
they will get wings
like eagles: running,
they will not be tired,
and walking, they will
have no weariness.

ISAIAH 40:31

Be strong
and take heart,
and have no fear of them;
for it is the Lord your God
who is going with you;
he will not take away
his help from you.

DEUTERONOMY 31:6

And those who have
knowledge of your name
will put their faith in you;
because you, Lord,
have ever given your help
to those who were
waiting for you.

PSALM 9:10

You will make clear
to me the way of life;
where you are joy
is complete; in
your right hand
there are pleasures
for ever and ever.

PSALM 16:11

God is our harbor and our strength, a very present help in trouble.

PSALM 46:1

When pride comes,
there comes shame,
but wisdom is with
the quiet in spirit.

PROVERBS 11:2

A friend
is loving
at all times,
and becomes a
brother in times
of trouble.

PROVERBS 17:17

And the Lord will be
your guide at all times;
in dry places he will
give you water in full
measure, and will make
strong your bones; and
you will be like a
watered garden, and like
an ever-flowing spring.

ISAIAH 58:11

So I say to you,
Take no thought
for your life, about food
or drink, or about clothing
for your body.
Is not life more than food,
and the body more
than its clothing?

MATTHEW 6:25

Make a request, and
it will be answered;
what you are searching
for you will get;
give the sign, and
the door will be
open to you.

MATTHEW 7:7

Greater love has
no man than this,
that a man
gives up his life
for his friends.

JOHN 15:13

You have been put to no test
but such as is common to man:
and God is true, who will not
let any test come on you which
you are not able to undergo;
but he will make with the test
a way out of it, so that you
may be able to go through it.

1 CORINTHIANS 10:13

Lord, by your grace
you have kept my
mountain strong:
when your face
was turned from me
I was troubled.

PSALM 30:7

For those who are living

in the way of the flesh

give their minds to the things

of the flesh, but those who go in the

way of the Spirit, to the things

of the Spirit. For the mind of

the flesh is death, but the mind

of the Spirit is life and peace.

ROMANS 8:5–6

Have no cares; but in
everything with prayer
and praise put your
requests before God.
And the peace of God,
which is deeper than
all knowledge, will keep
your hearts and minds
in Christ Jesus.

PHILIPPIANS 4:6-7

For God
did not give us
a spirit of fear,
but of power and
of love and of
self-control.

2 TIMOTHY 1:7

Be free from the
love of money and
pleased with the
things which
you have; for he
himself has said,
I will be with you
at all times.

HEBREWS 13:5

Let it be all joy to you, my brothers, when you undergo tests of every sort; Because you have the knowledge that the testing of your faith gives you the power of going on in hope.

JAMES 1:2-3

There is no fear in love:
true love has no room
for fear, because where fear
is, there is pain; and he
who is not free from fear is
not complete in love.

1 JOHN 4:18

*For which cause
we do not give way to
weariness; but though
our outer man is getting
feebler, our inner man is
made new day by day.*

2 CORINTHIANS 4:16

When you go through the waters, I will be with you; and through the rivers, they will not go over you: when you go through the fire, you will not be burned; and the flame will have no power over you.

ISAIAH 43:2

For I am conscious
of my thoughts
about you, says the Lord,
thoughts of peace
and not of evil, to give
you hope at the end.

JEREMIAH 29:11

And those who have knowledge of your name will put their faith in you; because you, Lord, have ever given your help to those who were waiting for you.

PSALM 9:10

O give praise
to the Lord,
for he is good:
for his mercy
is unchanging
for ever.

PSALM 118:29

Because you, brothers, were marked out to be free; only do not make use of your free condition to give the flesh its chance, but through love be servants one to another.

GALATIANS 5:13

My little children,

do not let our love be

in word and in tongue,

but let it be in act

and in good faith.

1 JOHN 3:18

So let your desire
be for wisdom :
if you have it, there
will be a future,
and your hope
will not be cut off.

PROVERBS 24:14

Jesus said to them,

I am the light of the world;

he who comes with me

will not be walking

in the dark but will have

the light of life.

JOHN 8:12

Now faith is
the substance of
things hoped for,
and the sign that
the things not seen
are true.

HEBREWS 11:1

And I will take the blind
by a way of which they had
no knowledge, guiding them
by roads strange to them:
I will make the dark places
light before them, and
the rough places level.
These things will I do
and will not give them up.

ISAIAH 42:16

By you my sorrow is turned into dancing; you have taken away my clothing of grief, and given me robes of joy.

PSALM 30:11

Say to those who
are full of fear,
Be strong and take
heart: see, your God
will give punishment; the
reward of God will
come; he himself will
come to be your savior.

ISAIAH 35:4

For everything
there is a fixed
time, and a time
for every business
under the sun.

ECCLESIASTES 3:1

But the Lord said
to Samuel, Do not
take note of his face or
how tall he is, because I will
not have him: for the Lord's
view is not man's; man takes
note of the outer form,
but the Lord sees the heart.

1 SAMUEL 16:7

For our present trouble,

which is only for a short time,

is working out for us a much

greater weight of glory;

While our minds are not on the

things which are seen, but on

the things which are not seen:

for the things which are seen are

for a time; but the things which

are not seen are eternal.

2 CORINTHIANS 4:17–18

And not only so, but let us have joy in our troubles: in the knowledge that trouble gives us the power of waiting; And waiting gives experience; and experience, hope: And hope does not put to shame; because our hearts are full of the love of God through the Holy Spirit which is given to us.

ROMANS 5:3–5

Two are better than one,
because they have a good
reward for their work.
And if one has a fall,
the other will give him a
hand; but unhappy is the
man who is by himself,
because he has no helper.

ECCLESIASTES 4:9–10

And let us
not get tired of
well-doing; for at the
right time we will get
in the grain, if we do not
give way to weariness.

GALATIANS 6:9

The first sign
of wisdom is to
get wisdom; go, give
all you have to get
true knowledge.

PROVERBS 4:7

Keep your eyes on
what is in front
of you, looking
straight before you.
Keep a watch on your
behavior; let all your ways
be rightly ordered.

PROVERBS 4:25–26

And we are conscious
that all things are
working together for
good to those who
have love for God,
and have been marked
out by his purpose.

ROMANS 8:28

Let all you

do be done

in love.

1 CORINTHIANS 16:14

As saints of God, then,
holy and dearly loved,
let your behavior be
marked by pity and
mercy, kind feeling, a low
opinion of yourselves,
gentle ways, and a power
of undergoing all things.

COLOSSIANS 3:12

And keep watch
over your heart
with all care;
so you will
have life.

PROVERBS 4:23

And you are to have
love for the Lord
your God with
all your heart, and
with all your soul,
and with all your
mind, and with all
your strength.

MARK 12:30

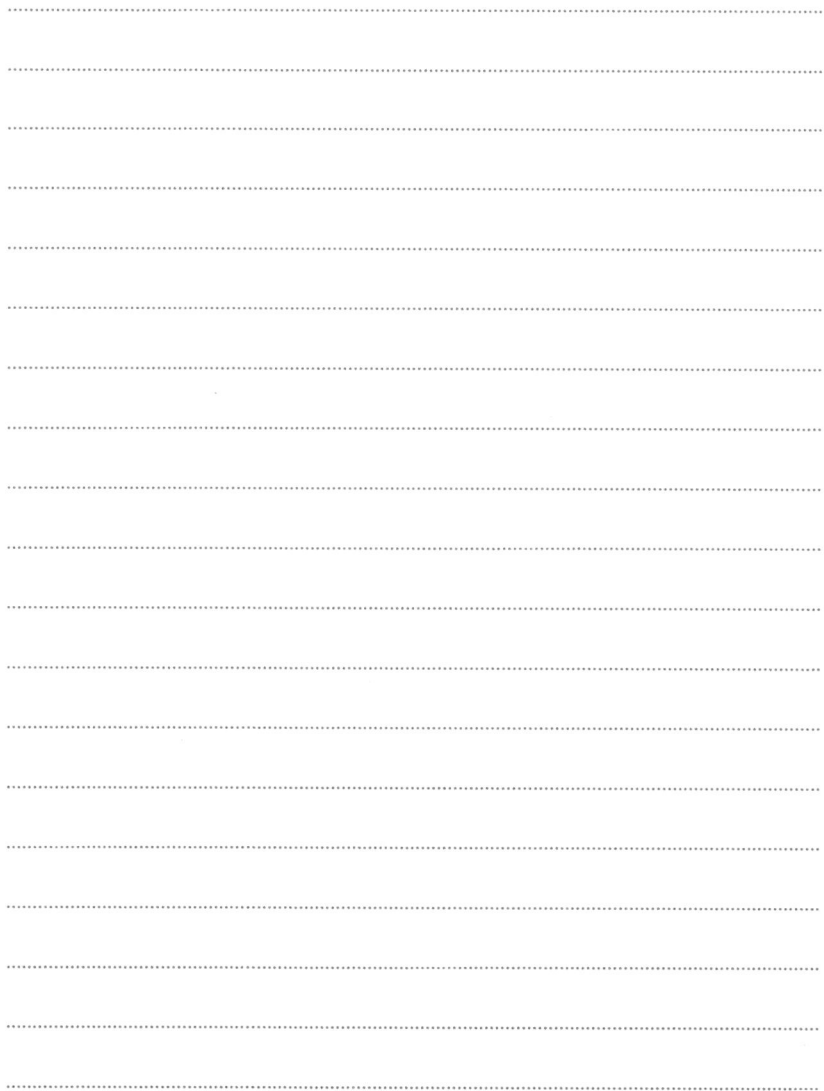

And the light goes

on shining in the dark;

it is not overcome

by the dark.

JOHN 1:5

He who goes about talking of others makes secrets public, but the true-hearted man keeps things covered.

PROVERBS 11:13

Not giving back
evil for evil, or curse
for curse, but in place
of cursing, blessing; because
this is the purpose of God
for you that you may have
a heritage of blessing.

1 PETER 3:9

Give, and it will
be given to you; good
measure, crushed down, full
and running over, they will
give to you. For in the same
measure as you give, it will
be given to you again.

LUKE 6:38

But I say to you who give ear
to me, Have love for those
who are against you, do good
to those who have hate for
you, Give blessing to those
who give you curses, say
prayers for those who are
cruel to you.

LUKE 6:27-28

Do to others as
you would have
them do to you.

LUKE 6:31

Then have no care
for tomorrow:
tomorrow will take
care of itself.
Take the trouble
of the day as it comes.

MATTHEW 6:34

Take part in the
joy of those who
are glad, and in the
grief of those who
are sorrowing.

ROMANS 12:15

Do not let your ornaments be those of the body such as dressing of the hair, or putting on of jewels of gold or fair clothing; But let them be those of the unseen man of the heart, the ever—shining ornament of a gentle and quiet spirit, which is of great price in the eyes of God.

1 PETER 3:3-4

Be not judges of others,
and you will not be judged:
do not give punishment to
others, and you will not get
punishment yourselves:
make others free, and you
will be made free.

LUKE 6:37

For if you let men
have forgiveness
for their sins, you will
have forgiveness
from your Father
in heaven.

MATTHEW 6:14

Be in harmony with
one another. Do not have
a high opinion of
yourselves, but be in
agreement with
common people.
Do not give yourselves
an air of wisdom.

ROMANS 12:16

Let no one make little
of you because you are
young, but be an example
to the church in word,
in behavior, in love, in
faith, in holy living.

1 TIMOTHY 4:12

The steps of a good man are

ordered by the Lord, and he

takes delight in his way.

Even if he has a fall he will not

be without help: for the hand of

the Lord is supporting him.

PSALMS 37:23-24

My son, give ear to the training of your father, and do not give up the teaching of your mother: For they will be a crown of grace for your head, and chain-ornaments about your neck.

PROVERBS 1:8–9

Truly, blessing and mercy will be with me all the days of my life; and I will have a place in the house of the Lord all my days.

PSALM 23:6

For the rest, my brothers,
whatever things are true, whatever
things have honor, whatever things
are upright, whatever things are
holy, whatever things are beautiful,
whatever things are of value,
if there is any virtue and if
there is any praise, give thought
to these things.

PHILIPPIANS 4:8

See how good

and how pleasing

it is for brothers

to be living together

in harmony!

PSALM 133:1

Great are

the troubles of the

upright: but the Lord

takes him safely out

of them all.

PSALM 34:19

The light of the eyes

is a joy to the heart,

and good news

makes the bones fat.

PROVERBS 15:30

It is the same to me
if I am looked down
on or honored; everywhere
and in all things I have the
secret of how to be full and
how to go without food;
how to have wealth and
how to be in need.

PHILIPPIANS 4:12

*Sorrow is better
than joy;
when the face
is sad, the
mind gets better.*

ECCLESIASTES 7:3

Let love be without deceit.
Be haters of what is evil;
keep your minds fixed
on what is good.
Be kind to one another
with a brother's love,
putting others before
yourselves in honor.

ROMANS 12:9-10

The man who has mercy
will be rewarded,
but the cruel man
is the cause of trouble
to himself.

PROVERBS 11:17

By a soft answer

wrath is turned away,

but a bitter word is a

cause of angry feelings.

PROVERBS 15:1

Care in the heart

of a man makes

it weighted down,

but a good word

makes it glad.

PROVERBS 12:25

I am able to do

all things through him

who gives me strength.

PHILIPPIANS 4:13

Have no fear, for
I am with you; do not be
looking about in trouble,
for I am your God;
I will give you strength, yes,
I will be your helper; yes,
my true right hand will be
your support.

ISAIAH 41:10

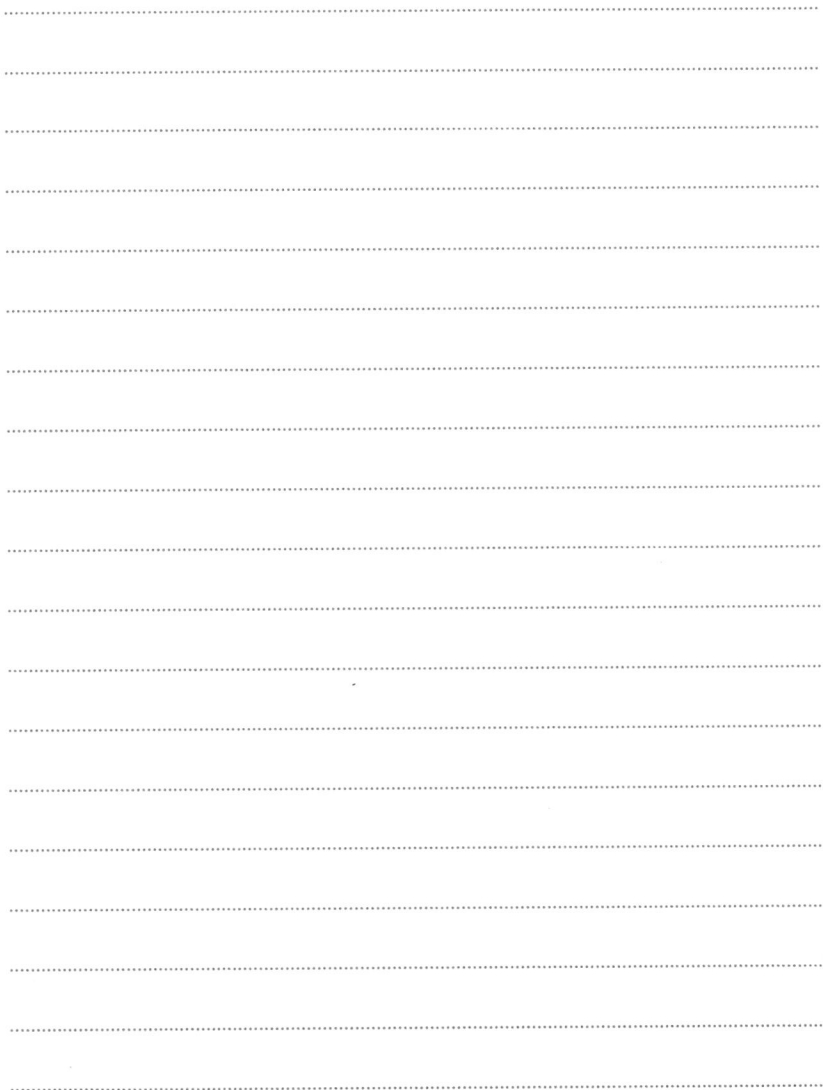

Have I not given you your orders?

Take heart and be strong;

have no fear and do not be

troubled; for the Lord your God

is with you wherever you go.

JOSHUA 1:9

And our desire is
that you will keep control
over those whose lives
are not well ordered,
giving comfort to the
feeble-hearted, supporting
those with little strength,
and putting up with
much from all.

1 THESSALONIANS 5:14

Take my yoke on you and become like me, for I am gentle and without pride, and you will have rest for your souls; for my yoke is good, and the weight I take up is not hard.

MATTHEW 11:29-30

Now may the God of hope make you full of joy and peace through faith, so that all hope may be yours in the power of the Holy Spirit.

ROMANS 15:13

So then, go on comforting and building up one another, as you have been doing.

1 THESSALONIANS 5:11

The Lord God is my strength,

and he makes my feet

like roes' feet, guiding me

on my high places.

For the chief music-maker

on corded instruments.

HABAKKUK 3:19

May peace be with you;

my peace I give to you: I give

it not as the world gives.

Let not your heart be troubled;

let it be without fear.

JOHN 14:27

For the word of God is living and full of power, and is sharper than any two-edged sword, cutting through and making a division even of the soul and the spirit, the bones and the muscles, and quick to see the thoughts and purposes of the heart.

HEBREWS 4:12

He has made clear
to you, O man,
what is good; and what is
desired from you by the Lord;
only doing what is right,
and loving mercy,
and walking without
pride before your God.

MICAH 6:8

The heart of the man
of good sense gets
knowledge; the ear of
the wise is searching
for knowledge.

PROVERBS 18:15

And let us be moving one
another at all times to love
and good works;
Not giving up our meetings,
as is the way of some, but
keeping one another strong in
faith; and all the more because
you see the day coming near.

HEBREWS 10:24–25

Keep your mind

on the

higher things,

not on the

things of earth.

COLOSSIANS 3:2

To give an answer

before hearing

is a foolish thing

and a cause of shame.

PROVERBS 18:13